Ravaud Kearney Rodgers

Historical Sketch of the Synod of New Jersey

A sermon preached at the opening of the Synod at Pottsville, Pa., October

15th, 1861

Ravaud Kearney Rodgers

Historical Sketch of the Synod of New Jersey
A sermon preached at the opening of the Synod at Pottsville, Pa., October 15th, 1861

ISBN/EAN: 9783337113995

Printed in Europe, USA, Canada, Australia, Japan

Cover: Foto ©Lupo / pixelio.de

More available books at **www.hansebooks.com**

HISTORICAL SKETCH

OF THE

SYNOD OF NEW-JERSEY.

———— ◆ ◆ ◆ ————

A SERMON

PREACHED AT THE

Opening of the Synod at Pottsville, Pa.,

OCTOBER 15th, 1861,

BY RAVAUD K. RODGERS, D. D.

PASTOR OF THE PRESBYTERIAN CHURCH,

BOUND BROOK, N. J.

AND MODERATOR OF THE SYNOD.

———— ◆ ◆ ————

PUBLISHED BY REQUEST OF THE SYNOD.

———— ◆ ◆ ————

New-Brunswick, N. J.

TERHUNE & VAN ANGLEN'S PRESS, ALBANY ST.

1861.

SERMON.

"And thou shalt remember all the way which the Lord thy God led thee."—Deut. viii : 2.

It is well to think on mercies past—to look back upon the way in which the Lord our God has led us —to call to mind the various blessings of a spiritual and temporal nature with which the Most High has been pleased to crown our years, and to contemplate his dealings with us under all the circumstances, in which, in his holy Providence we have been placed. Such a review with reference to ourselves or those in whom we may have been or are interested is often-times calculated to inspire us with confidence in God, and to lead us the more to cast our cares on him. If we are the professing followers of Jesus Christ, or are ambassadors of the Cross, and those circumstances have a bearing upon the church which he has established in our fallen world, and more especially upon that department of it with which we have the happiness to be connected, we shall find in them, the more that we ponder upon them, increasing reasons why we should make the Lord our trust. It was with the view of shewing the people of Israel what God had done for them, as well as for the purpose of keeping them in mind of the obligations which rested upon

them, arising from the many benefits which God had
kindly conferred, that the law-giver of Israel addressed them as he did in the words of the text.
The Israelites were, as it is well known, the peculiar
people of God—assurances of a very decided, and
we may add, of a very cheering character had been
given to the fathers that the blessings of the Most
High should not be withheld from the children, and
so long as there was a compliance on their part, with
the precepts of God's holy law, we find that light
was made to shine around them and deliverances
ofttimes of a remarkable character were wrought out
on their behalf. With all the circumstances of their
going down into Egypt—of their oppressions there
—of their wanderings in the wilderness, and of their
being about to be put in possession of the land which
God had promised to Abraham that his seed should
inherit it, you are all well acquainted. And it was
meet that they should remember with devout gratitude the mercies which had been so profusely scat-
tered all along the path in which they had been led.
But the people of Israel were not the only people for
whom the charge in the text was intended. True, it
was primarily addressed to them, but it is to be considered as addressed through them to us; and not to
notice the voice of the Most High, which is uttered
here, betrays an indifference in regard to great interests, and manifests a degree of ingratitude, with
which it is apprehended no one of us would be willing to be charged. What have we that we have
not received? In asking your attention then, Fathers
and Brethren of the ministry and eldership to the

charge in the text, on this occasion, it is my purpose to present some statements in connection with the history of the Synod with which we are more immediately connected, and from them we shall see how the Lord our God has led this Judicatory of our church, and that portion of Zion embraced in its limits. It has been, as we shall find, in many respects, a highly favored part of the heritage of Jacob, and it becomes us to remember what God has done for it, and for us, as belonging to it.

The Synod of New Jersey was originally a part of the Synod of New York and New Jersey, the first arrangements for the erection of which, were made by the Synod of New York and Philadelphia in the year 1786.* In 1787, the matter was again brought up and "the Synod agreed that the arrangement of the Presbyteries under four Synods should for the present remain as determined last year."† There the whole matter rested under a resolution that the division of the Synod, which it would seem had not been fully perfected, be postponed until next year, and that the Synod be then divided.‡ In the year 1788, a resolution was passed that the Synod be divided agreeably to an act made and provided for that purpose in the year 1786, and that the division should commence upon the dissolution of the Synod then in session.§ The four Synods into which the original body was divided, were the Synods of *Philadelphia, New York and New Jersey, Virginia and the*

---

* Records of the Presbyterian Church—page 524.   † Do. page 541.
‡ Records—page 541.   § Do. page 548.

Carolinas, and these embraced the whole Presbyterian church. Previous to the year 1823, in which year the *Synod of New Jersey* was organized, the Synods of *Pittsburgh, Kentucky, Albany, South Carolina and Ohio* had been erected.| In 1823 the original Synod of New York and New Jersey having been divided, this Judicatory took its place among its sister Synods, and has now been in existence for a period of thirty-eight years. Its first meeting was held in the First Presbyterian Church in the City of Newark, N. J., in October, 1823, and was opened with a sermon by the venerable and Rev. Dr. John Woodhull, of Freehold: the Rev. Dr. Alexander of blessed memory, was the first Moderator. The Synod then consiste l of the Presbyteries of *New Brunswick, Jersey, Newton* and *Susquehanna*—those of *Hudson, North River, Long Island* and *New York* remaining to constitute *the Synod of New York*.

The Presbytery of *New Brunswick* the oldest of those set off, to aid in the constitution of this Synod, was organized in New Brunswick on the 8th of August, 1738, in accordance with the direction of the Synod of Philadelphia, on the 26th of May of that year. The order of the Synod was, that "all to the northward and eastward of Maidenhead and Hopewell unto the Raritan river, including also Staten Island" with several congregations which are named and which still belong to the Presbytery of New Brunswick, should be erected into a Presbytery, "and that the said Presbytery be distinguished by

---

| Pittsburgh organized in 1802; Kentucky do. 1802; Albany do. 1803; South Carolina do. 1813; Ohio do. 1814.

the name of the Presbytery of New Brunswick": as such, it remains with us to this day.

At the meeting of the Synod of New York and New Jersey, in October, 1809, and of course a number of years previous to the erection of this Synod, the Presbytery of New York was divided, and that part of the Presbytery lying in the State of New Jersey, was thereafter to be known as the Presbytery of Jersey; and so continued until the year 1824, when as we shall presently see, it was divided into the Presbyteries of Newark and Elizabethtown.

The Presbytery of *Newton*, the third of those stated as set off for the purpose of constituting this Synod, was formed from the Presbytery of New Brunswick, in October, 1817, and was "composed of those members and congregations of the Presbytery of New Brunswick which lie north and west of a line drawn from the Delaware river so as to include the congregations of Amwell, Flemington, Lamington and Baskingridge."

This Presbytery held its first meeting at Mansfield, on the 18th day of November, 1817, when it was duly organized, and agreeably to its first report, consisted of fifteen members, with twenty-five congregations.

The Presbytery of *Susquehanna*, the last remaining *original* Presbytery of the Synod of New Jersey, was received under the care of the Synod of New York and New Jersey in the month of October, 1821.* This Presbytery had been known as *the Luzerne Association*, but, having unanimously adopted the con-

---

* Minutes of Synod, vol. 1, page 510.

fession of faith and book of discipline of the Presbyterian Church in the United States, requested to be received under the care of this Synod, provided that such of their churches as chose to do so, might be allowed to manage their own concerns in the congregational manner; and they were received under the plan of union of 1801, and such was the original constitution of the Synod of New Jersey. The whole number of ministers in connection with it, when erected, was *eighty-three,** and the whole number of churches *one hundred and four.* Of these eighty-three ministers, but *fourteen* are now living, so far as we can learn—*six* of them retaining their membership with this body—and these are all that are left with us, to tell us from actual experience, how the Lord our God has led the Synod of *New Jersey.* Verily, when we contemplate such a change as has taken place in the membership of this body, during the thirty-eight years of its existence, we are constrained to ask, "Our fathers, where are they? And the prophets, do they live forever?"† The *six* who yet remain are the Rev. Dr. KIRKPATRICK, who may well be regarded as the patriarch of the Synod, he having been engaged in the work of the ministry more than half a century, the Rev. Dr. PERKINS, the

	* MINISTERS.	CHURCHES.
New Brunswick,	24	16
Newton,	17	28
Jersey,	32	34
Susquehanna,	10	26
	83	104

† Dr. Kirkpatrick, ordained June 20th, 1810; Dr. Perkins, do. Dec. 6th, 1820; Dr. Magie, do. April 24th, 1821; Mr. Williamson, do. Nov. 6th, 1821; Dr. Hodge and Dr. Studdiford, do. Nov. 28th, 1821.

Rev. Dr. MAGIE, the Rev. Dr. HODGE, the Rev. Dr. STUDDIFORD and the Rev. Mr. ABRAHAM WILLIAMSON. As the thirty-eight years of the Synod's existence have been passing along, the Synod has increased from *four* to *eleven* Presbyteries—besides having had under its care still others to which reference will presently be made—from *eighty-three* to *one hundred and eighty five* ministers, and from *one hundred and four* churches to *one hundred and ninety-four*; so that if every minister should be in attendance and each church should be represented, as each church ought to be, we should have an assembly of *three hundred and seventy-nine* ministers and elders, to take part in the deliberations of the body. The number of ministers and churches thus stated is irrespective of those connected with the Presbytery of Corisco in Africa, that Presbytery not having made, when received under the care of the Synod, any report in regard to its number of ministers and churches, though we have since learned that they had *four* ministers and one church. But here it is our mournful duty to say that that small number of four has been diminished by the departure from life of the beloved missionary OGDEN, whom the Master has called to his home on high! As it respects the increase of *members* in the churches we cannot speak with any degree of accuracy, the reports of churches being from year to year, in many cases very defective. The reports of the Presbyteries to the last General Assembly make the number in connection with our churches to be twenty-three thousand eight hundred and twenty-three. By the reports of the several

Presbyteries to the Synod at the last stated meeting, there appear to be *twenty-seven* licentiates and *twenty three* candidates under their care.

We have stated that in the year 1824, the Presbytery of *Jersey* was divided into the Presbyteries of *Newark* and *Elizabethtown.* The Presbytery of *Newark* remained as one of the Presbyteries of this Synod until the year 1839, when it was disowned by the Synod and declared to be no longer in connection with it in consequence of its having declared its adherence to the body which went off from the General Assembly of 1838 and held its sessions in the First Presbyterian Church in Philadelphia, and which claimed to be, in the face of all law and order, the true General Assembly. The Presbytery of *Elizabethtown* remains with us to this day.

In the year 1832 the Presbytery of *Montrose* was erected, having been taken from the Presbytery of Susquehanna. It continued to be one of the Presbyteries of the Synod until the year 1838, when it was declared to be no longer in connection with it, it having by its own measures placed itself in an ecclesiastical connection inconsistent with any longer relation to this Synod.

The Presbytery of *Caledonia*, next in order of age, was erected in the year 1838. It was originally a part of the Presbytery of Susquehanna. This latter body occupying a territory of more than two hundred miles in extent, it was considered advisable that it should be divided. In accordance with the request of the Presbytery, *five* ministers and *five* churches were detached from it, and constituted into a Presbytery to be known as that of *Caledonia*. This Presbytery remained in connection with the Synod until the year 1843, constantly increasing in numbers and efficiency. Their last report was made in 1842, when they reported fifteen ministers and fourteen churches with one licentiate and two candidates under their care·

At the meeting of the Synod in 1842, this Presbytery preferred a request, in view of the extent of their territory and the fact that some ministers and churches from the disowned Synods in the State of New York had cast in their lot with them, for a division, and the two Presbyteries of *Steuben* and *Wyoming* were constituted—the name of Caledonia being dropped. In the month of May, 1843, the General Assembly erected the Synod of Buffalo, in accordance with the enactment of the Assembly of 1838, and attached these newly erected Presbyteries to that Synod,* the Presbytery of Ogdensburgh, before connected with the Synod of Albany, being detached from that Synod for the purpose of making up the number necessary for the formation of the new Synod.

Next in order is the Presbytery of *Raritan*, which was erected by this Synod in October, 1839, and organized on the 5th of November of that year. This Presbytery was taken, for the most part, from the Presbytery of Newton, and consisted at the outset of nine ministers and twelve churches from that Presbytery, and one minister and two churches from the Presbytery of New-Brunswick; and has since its organization, though among the smallest of our Presbyteries, been zealously engaged in founding churches

* Minutes of Assembly for 1843—page 174.

—repairing the waste places, and extending the interests of the Redeemer's Kingdom within its borders.

In the year 1843, the Presbytery of *Luzerne* was formed by the General Assembly,* the Committee of Bills and Overtures, having presented an overture to that effect. Two ministers and four churches were detached from the Presbytery of Susquehanna; two ministers and four churches from the Presbytery of Newton; one church from the Presbytery of Northumberland, and one from the Presbytery of Philadelphia. This Presbytery so constituted by the supreme judicatory of our church, was attached to this Synod. It was duly organized at Wilkesbarre, on the 19th of September of the same year. This Presbytery has had from the beginning, a very important missionary field within its borders, and by the blessing of the Head of the church upon the labors of those connected with it, has become one of the largest in our body—having reported at the last stated meeting twenty-four ministers and twenty-eight churches, with four licentiates and one candidate under their care.

At the same meeting of the General Assembly at which the Presbytery of *Luzerne* was constituted, the Presbytery of *West Jersey*,† which was organized in 1839, having been erected from the Presbytery of Philadelphia, was, in compliance with the petition of the Presbytery, set off from the Synod of Philadel-

---

* Minutes of Assembly, 1843—page 195.

† Minutes of Assembly, 1843—page 174.

phia, and attached to this Synod, and is now with us, laboring zealously in that part of the State of New Jersey, falling within its bounds, nor, if we are to judge of the results, have the smiles of the Master been withheld from the efforts they have made to advance the interests of his kingdom. Their number of ministers has increased from *twelve* to *seventeen*, and their churches from *fifteen* to *twenty two*, during the time of their connection with us, and that too, when ministers and churches have been taken from them to aid in the constitution of another Presbytery.

In the year 1849, the Presbytery of Burlington was formed from the Presbyteries of New-Brunswick and West Jersey, *three* ministers and *three* churches being taken from the former and *two* ministers and three churches from the latter. At the stated meeting of the Synod in 1851, with the view of strengthening this Presbytery, the church of Allentown, with its pastor, the Rev. Mr. (now Dr.) PERKINS was transferred from the Presbytery of New-Brunswick to that of Burlington, and at the stated meeting in 1859, at the instance of the lamented VAN RENSSELAIR, who took, as all well know, a deep interest in everything connected with the affairs of our church, the territory of the Presbytery of Burlington was extended so as to include within its bounds the city of Camden and the townships of Newton, Union, Centre and Delaware in the County of Camden, N. J. By this action of the Synod, the Rev. Dr. STEWART and the church of Camden, (for at that time there was but one Presbyterian Church in that city,) were detached from the Presbytery of West Jersey and set over to the

Presbytery of Burlington. This Presbytery, has, as
is the case with others in our bounds, a large missionary field committed to its care, and very earnest
efforts are being made to remove the obstacles in the
way of the growth of that kingdom which is not of
this world, and who that loves to pray "thy kingdom
come," will not ask that that which is done for the
upbuilding of Zion's cause within the borders of Burlington Presbytery, may be crowned with abundant
success!

The Presbytery next to be noticed as connected
with this Synod is that of *Passaic.* At the meeting
of the Synod in 1852, a memorial was presented by
the Presbytery of Elizabethtown for a division of
that Presbytery. The Committee of Bills and Overtures having reported favorably to the measure, the
Presbytery was divided, and a new Presbytery was
formed, to be known as the Presbytery of *Passaic.*
The Presbytery thus erected was duly organized at
Paterson, N. J., on the 10th of November of 1852,
and may be said to have commenced its existence
under very favorable auspices, having at the outset,
seventeen ministers and *fourteen* churches, and among
these are some of the largest, and most able and
influential in the Synod.

The Presbytery of Monmouth, the last constituted
by the Synod, was erected at the meeting of the Synod,
in the year 1859, and was organized at the Tennent
Church on the 11th of January, 1860. It was taken
wholly from the Presbytery of New-Brunswick, and
consisted at its organization of *twelve* ministers and
thirteen churches. This Presbytery has an important

missionary field commonly known as the *Pines* within
its bounds, and the manner in which the members of
this new organization have commenced their work,
furnishes ground for the hope that ere long the
wilderness, which it has fallen to their lot to cultivate,
may become a fruitful field, and their whole ecclesiastical enclosure as the garden of the Lord.

The only remaining Presbytery to be noticed as in
connection with this Synod is that of Corisco in
Africa, which was organized in the month of May,
1860,* and taken under the care of the Synod of
New Jersey, at their own request in October, 1860,
in accordance with the rule of the General Assembly
in such cases. One of the members† of that Presbytery being present, took his seat as a member of the
Synod. The organization of a Presbytery in that far
off and benighted land, is as a light shining in a dark
place and leads to the indulgence of the hope that
by the blessing of God upon the labors of the band
of self-denying and devoted missionaries who are
connected with that infant Presbytery, Ethiopia will
soon stretch forth her hands unto God! Already
they have reason to rejoice in a church of fifty-seven
members—God speed the day when their little one
shall become a thousand and their small one a strong
nation—a nation of believers, scattering the light of
grace on all around.

Thus we see that there have been under the care
of the Synod, since its erection in 1823, *seventeen*

16

Presbyteries,* of which *eleven* remain with us to this day; and who is there not prepared to say, when we compare the present condition of the Synod in point of *Presbyteries* and *ministers* and *churches* and *members*, with its Estate at its commencement, that the Lord our God has led us in a way of great mercy.

During the period to which we have been making allusion, to wit, from 1823 to 1860 inclusive, (for the reports of the year just closed, are yet to be made,) there have been, in the several Presbyteries while connected with the Synod, *two hundred and seventy-three ordinations* to the work of the ministry, the greater part of which were with a view to the pastoral office; *two hundred and thirty-six installations* of ministers who had been previously ordained. There have been *three hundred and eighty dismissions* of ministers from their respective Presbyteries to other Presbyteries or ecclesiastical bodies not immediately connected with our own church; *two hun-*

---

* PRESBYTERIES.	CONSTITUTED.	
New-Brunswick,	1738.	
Jersey,	1809.	Divided in 1824.
Newton,	1817.	
Susquehanna,	1821.	
Newark,	1824.	Disowned in 1839.
Elizabethtown,	1824.	
Montrose,	1832.	Disowned in 1838.
Caledonia,	1838.	Divided in 1842.
Steuben,	1842.	Attached to the Synod of
Wyoming,	1842.	Buffalo, in 1843.
Raritan,	1839.	
Luzerne,	1843.	
West Jersey,	1839.	
Burlington,	1849.	
Passaic,	1852.	
Monmouth,	1859.	
Corisco,	1860.	

dred and sixty-seven dissolutions of the pastoral relation have taken place; *four hundred and seventy*
persons have been licensed to preach the everlasting
Gospel; *one hundred and twenty-six churches* have
been organized, and *sixty-nine* of the *clerical members* of the Synod, without including those whom it
has pleased God to take away from among us during
the past year, have been removed by *death*, and of
this number, as all who have been acquainted with
the members of this Synod well know, were many
who might well be termed burning and shining lights
in our beloved Zion. We mourn to-day, in an
especial manner, the absence by reason of *death*, of
four of our members, *three* of whom while with us,
were prominent members of this body, and were in
attendance in the enjoyment of their usual health, at
the last stated meeting of the Synod. I allude to
the Rev. Dr. Isaac V. Brown,* of the Presbytery of
New-Brunswick, one of the oldest members of the
Synod, having been set apart to the work of the
ministry in the month of June, 1807. Dr. Brown
was the pastor of the church of Lawrence for twenty-
one years, and for a large part of that time, a successful teacher of youth. His relation to the church he
served, was dissolved in December, 1828, since which
time to the date of his death, he lived in comparative
retirement.

The Rev. Dr. Murray, the second of those to
whom I have referred, as taken from us by death
during the year, was suddenly removed, in February

---

* The Rev. Dr. Brown died at Trenton on the 19th of April, 1861, in the 78th
year of his age.

last, after a highly successful pastorate in the 1st
Church of Elizabethtown, for the period of nearly
twenty-eight years, he having been, previous to his
settlement among that people, the pastor of the church
in Wilkesbarre, where he was ordained and installed
in November, 1829. He removed from Wilkesbarre
to Elizabethtown in 1833, and was installed as pastor
of the 1st Church in the latter place in July, 1833.*
The name of NICHOLAS MURRAY is recorded as present
at every meeting of the Synod of New Jersey from
the meeting in 1830, the first held after his ordination,
to 1860, and such a record cannot be made of any
other individual so long connected with this body.
In this, our departed brother has set an example
which many would do well to follow. And here, I
am happy in being allowed to bear my testimony in
his behalf, in the language of his bereaved and
mourning co-presbyters, who knew him well, and
knew how to estimate his character and worth ;
"His name, his character and his works are already
on record, wide as the limits of the church at home
and abroad." "A willing worker, devising liberal
things, fraternally genial, decided in the faith and
order of our church, but no bigot nor sympathi er
with the exclusive." I regarded it my privilege to
be with those who accompanied his remains to their
resting-place in the midst of the great congregation

* Dr. Murray died on the 4th of February, 1861. Dr. Murray was licensed to
preach the Gospel by the Presbytery of Philadelphia, in April, 1829. For a
more extended notice of his life and labors, see the sermon, preached on the
occasion of his death, by the Rev. Dr. Sprague of Albany, on Sabbath, Feb. 10th,
1861. The sermon was preached at Elizabethtown, the Sabbath after Dr. Murray
died.

sleeping by the side of the Sanctuary where he so long ministered. Very pleasant was he to me! Sweet be his sleep on his pillow of dust!

The *third* stated to have been present at the last meeting of the Synod, and removed from toil on earth to reward on high, is the Rev. Dr. JOHN DORRANCE,* for many years a member of the Presbytery within the bounds of which we are now assembled, a brother greatly beloved. We do not wonder that brethren with whom he had been long associated and who knew him best, should deplore his loss, as that of a devoted friend, a wise and able counsellor, whose comprehensive mind and catholic spirit embraced the whole church, and whose constant exertions for more than a quarter of a century were devoted to the spiritual interests of the large missionary field within the bounds of the Presbytery with which he was connected. And his too was the privilege of enjoying a longer pastorate than usually falls to the lot, in these days of too frequent ministerial changes. He was installed the pastor of the church of Wilkesbarre on the 22nd of August, 1833. The church to which he so long ministered was happy in obtaining the services of one to go in and out before them, whose heart was in his work, so soon after the departure from among them of the lamented MURRAY, for their vacancy was scarcely of two months duration. But we shall see these brethren no more among us. The Master has done serving himself of them here, and they have gone away at his bidding to receive the welcome of the Judge, and the reward

---

* Dr. Dorrance died on the 18th of April, 1861.

of the good and faithful servant. The *fourth* spoken
of as removed by death since our last meeting, is one
in whom many fond hopes were centered, and in
regard to whom, hope was entertained that he might
be the instrument of great good to the benighted in
Africa, among whom as a foreign missionary he had
cast his lot. THOMAS SPENCER OGDEN, a son of one
who was long a member of this Synod, was set apart
to the work of the ministry as a missionary to the
heathen, by the Presbytery of New-Brunswick, on
the 18th of August, 1857, and was appointed by our
Foreign Board to labor in *Corisco* in Africa.* He
had begun his work with the pleasant prospect of
usefulness, but He, who seeth not as man seeth, was
pleased to call him to an higher sphere at a time
when to human view it was necessary for him to
abide in the flesh. He died on the 12th of May last,
with an abiding trust in Him who had called him to his
work. "In whom else can we trust," said the youth-
ful missionary, in his dying hour, when asked by one
who stood by his couch, if he found comfort in trust-
ing in Christ? The removal from the Synod during
the thirty-eight years of its existence of *seventy-three*
of its members by death, is a loud and solemn call to
us who survive, to be preparing for the season when
the Master shall be pleased to call us away from our
loved work in his church below. But four of these
thirty-eight years have gone by without report having
been made that death had entered the Sanctuary of
God, and summoned hence the ambassador of the

* Mr. Ogden left New York on the 6th of October, 1857, and reached Corisco
on the 14th of January, 1858, and entered at once upon his work and that with
a zeal which shewed that he was in earnest.

cross. The highest number called away in any one year was *seven* and that was from October 1859 to October 1860; of these *four* were taken from the Presbytery of *New-Brunswick*, and *one* from each of the Presbyteries of *West Jersey*, *Luzerne* and *Burlington*.

But, my brethren, while the Most High has been going forth among us in the *judgments* of his hands, and doing his strange work, he has been leading us as a body in ways of *great mercy*. This Synod has been a highly favored part of the heritage of the Lord. Very many of the churches under our care have reason to speak forth the praise of the Lord. They have not been without manifest tokens of the Divine presence. We do not know of a single year of the Synod's existence having passed away in which there has not been reference to the gracious dealings of God in the way of revivals in some part of our field. At one time, the grace of the Master has been like the gentle dew diffusing its tender influence and causing the plants of grace to grow and thrive. At another, it has been like the copious rain watering the dry and thirsty ridges of Zion, and making it to appear beyond all controversy that she is a field which the Lord has blessed. Yes, brethren, during these thirty-eight years precious revivals have been experienced, and thousands, through their holy and benign influence have begun their et·rnal song; and other thousands brought into the kingdom of God, as the result of the outpouring of the spirit and laboring to extend his interests in the world, are waiting with patience the Master's call to come away from earth and unite with those who have gone before them in singing the praises of redeeming love, beside the throne on high. Who then that is called of God to the work of the ministry, and to whom has been committed the care of precious souls will not regard it his sweet privilege to labor for the descent of the Spirit upon and among those to whom he is called to break the bread of life. The remembrance of past revivals with their rich results, should encourage us to pray, Wilt thou not revive us again, that thy people may rejoice in thee? As it respects this matter, the Lord our God has led the churches of this Synod in a way of great mercy— for there are very few of them, that may not look back upon some period of their existence and call to mind the rich exhibitions of Divine power and grace in the upbuilding of Zion—in the strengthening the faith of believers and in the conversion of sinners unto God.

We have referred to the missionary field within the bounds of this Synod, the one usually known as the *Pines* in the State of New Jersey, stretching along its Atlantic shore, and within the bounds of the Presbyteries of *Monmouth, Burlington* and *West Jersey*; and the other embracing what are commonly called the *Coal Fields* in the State of Pennsylvania, under the care of the Presbyteries of *Luzerne* and *Susquehanna.* The Board of Domestic Missions in their last report state that forty-six* missionaries or

---

* MISSIONARY PASTORS.

New-Brunswick,	-	-	2	Luzerne, -	-	-	13
Elizabethtown,	-	-	2	West Jersey,	-	-	9
Passaic,	-	-	1	Burlington,	-	-	3
Newton,	-	-	5	Susquehanna,	-	-	6
Raritan,	-	-	2	Monmouth,	-	-	3
Total,	-	-	-	-	-	-	46

missionary pastors have been aided by the Board during the year ending March 1st, 1861. Of these, fifteen were within the three Presbyteries first named,* and nineteen within the bounds of the other two,† leaving twelve to be divided among the other five Presbyteries of the Synod, for the Presbytery of Corisco is under the immediate care of the Foreign Board. By the same report it appears that up to the date already mentioned, there had been contributed to the Board by the churches of the Synod, the sum of six thousand two hundred and seventy-eight dollars and fifty-one cents, and that for the support of the forty-six aided, there had been drawn from the Treasury, six thousand eight hundred and three dollars and ninety-nine cents, thus shewing that the sum of five hundred and twenty-four dollars and ninety-nine cents over and above what had been contributed had been paid by the Board for the purpose of sustaining the Gospel in feeble churches within our bounds; thus placing the Synod of New Jersey among the number of those who draw out more than they put into the Treasury of the Board for Domestic Missionary purposes. May I not say, that this ought not so to be? It is true that the monies which are given to the Board are not given for any particular church or Presbytery, but for the purpose of assisting churches which have not sufficient strength to sustain the Gospel. Still, it would be well if our churches would contribute a sufficient amount to sustain the ordinances of our holy religion in our needy

---

* Monmouth, Burlington and West Jersey.
† Luzerne and Susquehanna.

churches and leave a surplus for more distant portions of Zion. As it respects *benevolent contributions*, the churches of this Synod have, in the general, manifested a disposition to do their part in sustaining the agencies of the church. But two, out of the twenty-one Synods stated to be in connection with the Domestic Missionary office in Philadelphia, have during the year ending March 1st, 1861, paid in more money to the Treasury than the Synod of New Jersey, and these are the Synods of New York and Philadelphia, which include some of the largest and most wealthy churches in our whole communion. The contributions to the Foreign Board for the past year amounted to $8,128 43; to the Board of Education $2,652 76; to the Board of Publication $1,362 81; for the Church Extension Committee $1,386 47; making in all for these five Boards, the sum of $19,808 98; and if we add to this the monies collected in our churches for the disabled ministers fund, we shall have an aggregate of more than $20,000 during the year. To this we may further add the sums collected in the various churches for the *Bible, Tract, Sunday School* and *other institutions* not immediately under the control of our church, and we may safely estimate the collections of the year at $25,000.

But lest I should exhaust your patience by these already lengthened remarks, we shall close this discourse, by observing,

First, That we should remember the way which the Lord our God has led us *with devout gratitude* to the Great Head of the church, for the rich blessings with which it has pleased Him to crown this Synod.

during the thirty-eight years of its existence. And surely if any part of our American Zion is called upon to manifest feelings of gratitude it is that portion of it, with which we have the happiness to be connected. The Lord has done great things for us, whereof we are glad "Oh, magnify the Lord with me, and let us exalt his name *together!*" But,

Secondly, We should remember the way which the Lord our God has led us, *with deep humility and self-abasement.* We have been living, Fathers and Brethren, in a wonderful age of the church, and yet how little have we done! Nay, we may ask, what have we done for Him that died? God give us grace to humble ourselves before him and to lie low in the dust in view of our unfaithfulness! And then,

Finally, Let us remember the way which the Lord our God has led us, *with an holy determination in the strength of our Master, to manifest more fidelity during the time we shall be spared to labor in the church on the earth.* Our days, how swift they pass away! Those with whom we have taken sweet counsel are passing away with them. Let us work then while it is called to-day, that when the Master shall come and call for us, we may be prepared to render our account and to receive the welcome, "Well done good and faithful servants, enter ye into the joy of the Lord." Then Brethren, beloved in the bonds of the Gospel, as we have associated together in labors and toils on the earth, we shall dwell together in the presence of God where there is fulness of joy, and at his right hand where there are pleasures forevermore!

FIRST PRESBYTERIAN CHURCH, CAMDEN, N. J.
Corner Stone laid June 22, 1871.   Dedicated June 1, 1873.

HISTORICAL SKETCH

OF THE

SYNOD OF NEW JERSEY

FOR THE QUARTER OF A CENTURY,

FROM 1861 TO 1886.

A DISCOURSE

DELIVERED IN THE

FIRST PRESBYTERIAN CHURCH OF CAMDEN, N. J.,

AT THE

OPENING OF THE SYNOD, OCTOBER 18TH, 1886,

BY THE MODERATOR,

REV. ALLEN H. BROWN.

PUBLISHED BY REQUEST OF THE SYNOD.

PHILADELPHIA:
THE JAS. B. RODGERS PRINTING CO.,
52 and 54 North Sixth Street.
1888.

HISTORICAL DISCOURSE.

HITHERTO HATH THE LORD HELPED US.—1 Samuel 7: 12.

The Prophet Samuel called upon the people of Israel, to put away their strange gods, and they obeyed his voice, and put away Baalim and Ashtaroth, and served the Lord only.

As they assembled at Mizpeh to worship by sacrifice and prayer, with confession of sin, the armies of the Philistines attacked them : but the Lord thundered upon their enemies and discomfited them. Then Samuel took a stone and set it between Mizpeh and Shen, and called the name of it EBENEZER (the stone of help), saying, Hitherto hath the Lord helped us.

History often repeats itself. Profitable it might be to illustrate how God chastens and humbles His people when they depart from Him, and how He delivers them when they return and confess their sins : but we must upon this occasion hasten to another application of the text.

Often when we take a retrospect of our own personal experience, or of the history of the Church of Christ, we are called again and again to raise a monument to God's mercy, and to inscribe upon it, " Hitherto hath the Lord helped us ;" and so will we do this day.

In 1874, or twelve years ago, the Synod of New Jersey, in session in this same First Church of the City of Camden, accepted the resignation of its Stated Clerk and Treasurer, the Rev. Ravaud K. Rodgers, D. D., with emphatic recognition of this remarkable fact, that for thirty-six years he had held the office, and discharged the duties of Stated Clerk and

5

Treasurer to the entire satisfaction of Synod, and that for more than forty years he had been a member of this body, and during all that time had never failed to be present, from the opening to the close of every meeting, though often meeting in distant places. *

At Pottsville, Pa., the same Doctor Rodgers, as Moderator, preached the opening sermon, from the text, Deuteronomy 8 : 2, "Thou shalt remember all the way, which the Lord thy God hath led thee," and presented a historical sketch of the Synod of New Jersey, from its organization in 1823 to that date, October 15th, 1861.

Concurrent and co-incident events suggest to your Moderator, about to retire, that it is timely, as he is filling out the fortieth year of labor in your missionary field, to take up the narrative and to give an outline of the history of the Synod of New Jersey for another quarter of a century, from 1861 to 1886, or at least to furnish additional materials for some later historian to finish the work ; believing that again and again in our experience as a Synod, we shall have occasion to apply the words of the text, and to say, "Hitherto hath the Lord helped us."

Accepting as correct the data and conclusions which Doctor Rodgers gave us in 1861, and limiting our investigation to the subsequent twenty-five years, it is nevertheless expedient to recall some well-known facts of antecedent history, e. g., that the First Presbytery was organized in 1705 or 6 ; that the Synod of Philadelphia began in 1717, and was divided in 1741 into two Synods; that these two Synods were reunited in 1758 under the name of the Synod of New York and Philadelphia; and that the first General Assembly met on the third Thursday of May 1789, when the whole Presbyterian Church comprised four Synods, viz., The Synod of Philadelphia ; The Synod of New York and New Jersey ; The Synod of Virginia, and The Synod of the Carolinas.

From the second of those four Synods, i. e., from the Synod

* See the Minutes of Synod, 1874, pp. 21 and 22.

of New York and New Jersey was the Synod of New Jersey organized in 1823, when it included four Presbyteries, viz., New Brunswick, Jersey, Newton, and Susquehanna. Its first meeting was held in the First Presbyterian Church, of Newark, in October, 1823. It was opened with a sermon by Doctor John Woodhull, of Freehold. Doctor Archibald Alexander was the first Moderator.

Doctor Rodgers gives a list of seventeen* Presbyteries, which had been under the care of the Synod of New Jersey. Six of the seventeen, viz., Jersey, Caledonia, Steuben, Wyoming, Montrose and Newark, were not on the roll of the Synod of New Jersey in 1861, Because:

The Presbytery of Jersey had been divided in 1824 into the Presbyteries of Newark and Elizabethtown, and the name Jersey had been dropped from the roll.

Caledonia was divided in 1842 into the two Presbyteries of Steuben and Wyoming, and the name Caledonia was also dropped. In 1843 the General Assembly attached these two Presbyteries, Steuben and Wyoming, to the Synod of Buffalo. †

Montrose Presbytery was removed from the Synod of New Jersey by the division of 1838, and Newark, also, until 1870.

* Seventeen Presbyteries under the care of Synod.

NAMES.	WHEN CONSTITUTED.	
New Brunswick,	1738	
Jersey,	1800	Divided in 1824.
Newton,	1817	
Susquehanna,	1821	
Newark,	1821	
Elizabethtown,	1824	
Montrose,	1832	
Caledonia,	1838	Divided in 1842.
Steuben,	1842	Attached to Synod of
Wyoming,	1842	Buffalo in 1843.
Raritan,	1839	
Luzerne,	1843	
West Jersey,	1839	
Burlington,	1849	
Passaic,	1852	
Monmouth,	1859	
Corisco,	1860	

† Minutes of General Assembly, 1843, p. 174.

Therefore, the names Jersey, Caledonia, Steuben and Wyoming, Montrose and Newark (for the present), are dismissed from our inquiry, because no one of them was on our roll in 1861, and the territory of most of them belongs to the State and Synod of Pennsylvania.

The remaining eleven Presbyteries in connection with the Synod of New Jersey in 1861 were Susquehanna, Luzerne, New Brunswick, Elizabethtown, Raritan, West Jersey, Burlington, Passaic, Monmouth, and Corisco.   Newton.

The Presbytery of Susquehanna, previously known as the Luzerne Association, was received under the care of the Synod of New York and New Jersey in 1821. Largely from its territory the Presbytery of Luzerne was constituted in 1843. Now, since the territory of both Susquehanna and Luzerne lies wholly in Pennsylvania, further notice of these must be relegated to the future historian of the Synod of Pennsylvania, while we restrict our present inquiry to the territory which the Synod of New Jersey now occupies, although the boundaries and the names of the constituent Presbyteries have been greatly changed.

Therefore, having dismissed with brief mention eight of the seventeen Presbyteries, the nine others connected with the Synod twenty-five years ago, viz.: New Brunswick, Newton, Elizabethtown, Raritan, West Jersey, Burlington, Passaic, Monmouth and Corisco together with the changes resultant from the reunion of 1870 claim our immediate and special attention.

PRESBYTERY OF NEW BRUNSWICK, INCLUDING RARITAN.

First and foremost, stands the old historic Presbytery of New Brunswick. Upon a supplication from some members of the Presbytery of New York to be erected into a distinct Presbytery with some of the members of the Presbytery of Philadelphia overtured that their petition be granted, &c.*

The original order of the Synod of Philadelphia † made

---

* Records Pres. Ch., p. 136.   † Records Pres. Ch., p. 136.

the bounds of the Presbytery of New Brunswick to be: All to the Northward and Eastward of Maidenhead (now Lawrenceville) and Hopewell (now Pennington) unto Raritan River, including Staten Island, Piscatua, Amboy, Bound Brook, Basking Ridge, Turkey, (now New Providence), Rocksiticus (now Mendham), Minisinks, Pequally, and Crosswicks, to be designated by the name of New Brunswick, to meet on the second Tuesday of August, 1738, at New Brunswick.

Gilbert Tennent, John Cross, Eleazer Wales, William Tennent, Samuel Blair were the original members from the Presbytery of New York.* At an earlier session of the same meeting of Synod in 1738, the Presbytery of New York had been constituted by the union of the members of East Jersey Presbytery with those of Long Island Presbytery.†

The Presbytery of New York at its organization in 1738 included in New Jersey the churches of Woodbridge, Hanover, Elizabethtown, Westfield, Newark and Connecticut Farms.‡

The Presbytery of New Brunswick encircling the College and Seminary of Princeton, and holding them as its peculiar treasure has always occupied a central and commanding position, and as in 1861, so it is now, the largest among the Presbyteries of Synod in the number of ministers. Its present territory includes Mercer county, with portions of Middlesex, and Hunterdon. In two more years this, the oldest Presbytery in the State, will have existed a century and a half, and then the 150th anniversary of its birth will be worthy of an appropriate commemoration.

PRESBYTERY OF RARITAN.—In 1870 the Presbytery of Raritan was merged in the Presbytery of New Brunswick and New Brunswick became the legal successor to Raritan. The Presbytery of Raritan was organized in 1839 with nine min-

---

* See Dr. Hall's History of the Presbyterian Church of Trenton, p. 132.
† See Dr. Hall's History, p. 19, and Records of Pres. Church, pp. 101, 134, 136.
‡ See History of the Presbytery of New York, p. 9, by S. D. Alexander, D. D.

isters and fourteen churches, largely from the Presbytery of
Newton.* The names of some of its prominent ministers and
churches will help to identify its position. Among its Pastors were Kirkpatrick, Studdiford, Olmstead, Campbell, and
H. W. Hunt, and among its churches, Amwell United First,
Amwell Second, Lambertville, Flemington, Pleasant Grove.
During the thirty years of its existence its ministers increased
from nine to nineteen : its churches from fourteen to eighteen
and the number of its communicants was nearly doubled.

PRESBYTERY OF NEWTON.

The Presbytery of Newton, next to New Brunswick the
oldest in the State, was composed of those members and congregations of the Presbytery of New Brunswick, which lie
north and west of a line drawn from the Delaware River so
as to include the congregations of Amwell, Flemington, Lamington and Basking Ridge, and extended also into Pennsylvania. It included originally some of the territory which
was subsequently transferred to the Presbytery of Raritan.
It now comprises the counties of Sussex and Warren and a
small portion of Hunterdon County.

In 1867 the Presbytery of Newton celebrated its semi-
centennial, when the Rev. D. X. Junkin gave an exhaustive
history, which was published in a pamphlet of one hundred
and six pages. From a review of statistics and narratives
the conclusion is irresistible that the Presbytery of Newton,
nestled amid her beautiful hills and lovely valleys, with an
endowed institution for the education of her sons and daughters,
is in proportion to population better supplied with Presbyterian Church accommodations than any other equal portion
of the State and, in comparison with other Presbyteries, has
in unwonted degree, enjoyed the dews of Divine Grace and
large accessions to its roll of communicants.

---

* D. X. Junkin's History of Newton Presbytery, pp. 16 and 17.

PRESBYTERY OF ELIZABETHTOWN, INCLUDING ELIZABETH.

By the division of the old Presbytery of Jersey into the Presbyteries of Elizabethtown and Newark the Presbytery of Elizabethtown was constituted in 1824.

The names of some churches will indicate the extent and influence of the Presbytery of Elizabethtown. In 1861 it had on its roll of churches, Elizabethtown First, Rahway First, Rahway Second, Woodbridge First, Basking Ridge, Plainfield First, Metuchen First. In 1870 it had only one more church than in 1825. A reason for its apparently small increase will appear hereafter in a notice of the organization of the Presbytery of Passaic.*

THE PRESBYTERY OF ELIZABETH in 1870 became the legal successor to the Presbytery of Elizabethtown. Its territory is now mainly in Union and Somerset Counties and a portion of Hunterdon along the line of the New Jersey Central Railroad. A knowledge of its historic churches may be obtained from Doctor Hatfield's exhaustive history of Elizabethtown.

PRESBYTERY OF WEST JERSEY.

The Presbytery of West Jersey organized in 1839 is already preparing to commemorate its semi-centennial. Some of the members of the Presbytery of Philadelphia, desirous of a separate organization, on several occasions brought the subject before the Synod of Philadelphia, but that body declined at each time to entertain the proposal. At length, they determined to present their case by a petition to the General Assembly of 1839. This petition having been placed in the hands of the Committee on Overtures, they declined reporting the subject to the General Assembly on the ground that the constitutional course would be, first, to lay the case before the Synod of Philadelphia for their action upon it. Accordingly, the substance of the petition was again brought before the Synod of Philadelphia in October, 1839. After discussion and opposition it was resolved to grant the request. On the

* See pp. 16 and 17.

5th of November, 1839, the Presbytery of West Jersey was organized with ten ministers and thirteen churches.*

The Synod of Philadelphia refused to concur in an application to the General Assembly, to transfer the Presbytery to the Synod of New Jersey, but the General Assembly of 1843 granted the petition of the Presbytery of West Jersey to be set off from the Synod of Philadelphia and attached to the Synod of New Jersey.†

Since 1870 its territory has been limited to the six southern counties of the State, or all south of Burlington county. Notwithstanding a diminution of territory and consequent surrender of some churches, the Presbytery has increased since its organization three and one-half fold, thus proving the wisdom of its separation from metropolitan oversight.

PRESBYTERY OF MONMOUTH, INCLUDING BURLINGTON.

The next in order of organization among extant Presbyteries is Monmouth, which dates from 1859. It became in 1870 the legal successor to the Presbytery of Burlington and absorbed its territory. The two Presbyteries are not identical, yet their history is closely identified.

Monmouth Presbytery was formed wholly from New Brunswick Presbytery in 1859, with twelve ministers and twelve or thirteen churches. It now comprises the counties of Monmouth, Ocean and Burlington, with some churches on the line of the Camden and Amboy Railroad in Middlesex and Mercer Counties. By reconstruction and active missionary effort it has increased nearly four-fold in twenty-five years. It has a large missionary field which it has diligently cultivated, thus justifying the design for which it was originally constituted.

THE PRESBYTERY OF BURLINGTON was formed in 1849 from the Presbyteries of New Brunswick and West Jersey. It was strengthened in 1851 by the addition of Allentown and in 1859 by adding the city of Camden. Doctor Cortland

---

* Pres. West Jersey Records, Vol. I, pp. 1-7.
† Min. G. A. 1843, p. 174.

Van Rensselaer was the father of this Presbytery. Being a small body, it was able to visit its small churches. In the twenty-one years of its existence the ministers of Burlington Presbytery increased from six to eleven; its churches from eight to fourteen and its communicants from 199 to 1190. Its more complete history is worthy of preparation and preservation. In 1870 the greater part of its territory was transferred to the Presbytery of Monmouth.

PRESBYTERY OF CORISCO.

The one other Presbytery which was on the roll of Synod twenty-five years ago is Corisco. In the statistical tables of the General Assembly the Presbytery of Corisco appears for the first time in the Minutes of 1861. Doctor Nassau in his Historical Sketch says that it was organized about 1859. Doctor Rodgers says in May, 1860, and that it was taken under the care of the Synod of New Jersey at their own request in October, 1860. (He refers to the Minutes of General Assembly, 1838, p. 42 and to Baird's Digest of 1856, p. 365.)

A mission had been established on the island of Corisco by our Presbyterian Board in 1850 and was successfully extended northward. Eight years previously (in 1842) a mission had been located in the estuary of Gaboon, under the American Board of Commissioners, which after many reverses was finally in 1870 formally transferred to the Presbyterian Board for Foreign Missions and incorporated with the Corisco Mission, whose official name was then changed to the Gaboon and Corisco Mission. That Mission of the American Board in the Gaboon District in 1842 was really a transfer of a Mission begun eight years before at Cape Palmas, where Messrs. Wilson, Walker, and Bushnell had labored. Manifestly, there is an unwritten history of toil, suffering and sacrifice, during another quarter of a century from 1834 to 1860, antedating and preparing the way for the Presbytery of Corisco, which now supervises all the churches in our Mission on the West coast of Africa, near the equator.

Ogove district was occupied in 1874 and progress has been made along the Ogove River into the interior.

So many sons and daughters have gone from beloved homes in New Jersey : so many have sacrificed their lives for the redemption of Africa : so many bound to you by the tenderest ties of kindred and affection are now enduring the greatest trials, as your special representatives to the heathen in that far distant land, that Corisco, the smallest and the weakest among the sisterhood of Presbyteries, must not be forgotten. Surely she has not been placed under the care of this Synod merely as a formal ecclesiastical convenience, but rather to claim our special sympathy and protection.

The regularity of its Presbyterial reports to the Synod and to the Assembly, and the columns in its statistical tables often well filled with contributions to all the Boards of the Church in this country, are worthy of notice and praise. Labors expended under great privation have not been in vain as the Narratives of Synod year by year attest, e. g.   In 1868,* thirty new members were reported to have joined the catechumen class in one church.   Again in 1872† in one of the churches there had been a continued revived state among the Christians and a deep religious interest among the heathen and as the result, twenty-five converts were added to the Lord. At the same time Presbytery reported as under its care five Candidates for the ministry.   Again the Narrative of 1876 said one-sixth of the entire membership belonging to the Presbytery of Corisco has been added on confession of faith during the past year and mentions many other tokens of encouragement.‡   Your Narrative of 1879 said, the far away Presbytery of Corisco sends the most encouraging report of all the Presbyteries of this Synod.‖

In recent years the work has been prosecuted under peculiar difficulties, due largely to the obstructions placed in the way

---

* See Minutes of Synod, 1868, p. 10.
† Ibid. 1872, p. 31.
‡ Ibid. 1876, pp. 38, 39.
‖ Ibid. 1879, p. 48.

by the French rulers of the coast. Verily, Corisco claims our more abundant sympathy and more earnest prayers that those obstacles may be removed and that a highway may be opened for the Gospel along the Ogove River to the very heart of Africa. Although a broad ocean rolls between us, the names Corisco, Benita, Baraka, Ogove, Kangwe, Talaguga, send a thrill of joy, or a pang of sorrow to many hearts and homes in the Synod of New Jersey. *

CHANGES BY RECONSTRUCTION.

In 1870 reconstruction revolutionized the Synod. A large portion of its territory was transferred to the Synod of Pennsylvania and an important accession was gained by the coming in of Newark and Rockaway, and two entirely new Presbyteries were formed. The one was Jersey City and the other was Morris and Orange, the latter including the previously existing Presbyteries Passaic and Rockaway.

PRESBYTERY OF NEWARK.

As already stated, Newark Presbytery was constituted with its twin sister Elizabethtown by the division of the old Presbytery of Jersey in 1824, and is therefore only one year younger than the Synod itself.

The Presbytery of Newark has been a part of the Synod of New Jersey with the exception of the period from 1838 to 1870, during which it belonged to the Synod of New York and New Jersey. Its territory was large as the names of some of its churches will indicate. The strength which it added to the Synod of New Jersey will more fully appear by a glance at its roll in 1870 when it reported fifty-eight ministers, thirty-five churches, 8,104 communicants who gave for congregational purposes $138,444. It then had in the city of Newark nine churches, including two German and one colored church, besides Madison, Orange First and Second ;

---

*See also Dr. Aikman's Report in Minutes of Synod 1883, pp. 37 and 39.

South Orange; Morristown South Street; Paterson Second; Caldwell, Plainfield, Elizabeth Third, and Montclair, each with a membership of from 200 to 510, and these twenty churches reporting 6,667 members, or an average of 333 members each. Now, with a smaller and compact territory Newark Presbytery exerts an influence inferior to none.

PRESBYTERY OF JERSEY CITY.

The Presbytery of Jersey City, constituted in 1870, comprises the counties of Bergen, Passaic, and Hudson. It has thirty-eight ministers and twenty-nine churches. Its strongest churches are in Englewood, Paterson and Jersey City. Including these places and Hoboken it has a large field, with a large German element, and it has very diligently prosecuted the work of church extension.

PRESBYTERY OF MORRIS AND ORANGE, INCLUDING PASSAIC AND ROCKAWAY.

Last upon our present roll and not least among our Presbyterial tribes is Morris and Orange. Beautiful for situation, this Presbytery enjoys and combines the wealth and refinement of the city with the pleasures and virtues of country life. In 1881, the beloved Dr. David Irving reviewed the progress of this Presbytery in a decennial discourse, which was published. At its organization in 1870 the Presbytery of Morris and Orange became the legal successor to the two Presbyteries, Passaic and Rockaway, which must now be noticed.

THE PRESBYTERY OF PASSAIC was formed out of the Presbytery of Elizabethtown by the Synod of New Jersey in 1852, and was organized in Paterson, November 10th of that year. It began with seventeen ministers and fourteen churches. Some of these were among the largest of the parent Presbytery, such as Elizabethtown Second, Newark Third, Morristown First, Morristown Second, Paterson First, and Connecticut Farms. These six churches had 1959' members, or an average of 326 each. This Presbytery reported in 1870 twenty-nine ministers and nineteen churches and 3662 members. One should add the statistics of this Passaic Presbytery in 1870 to those of Elizabeth in order to estimate the growth of the parent Presbytery, Elizabethtown, in the previous eighteen years.

PRESBYTERY OF ROCKAWAY.—By the General Assembly meeting in the First Church of Philadelphia in 1839, it was ordered to divide the Presbytery of Newark, and to erect the Presbytery of Rockaway to meet at Parsippany on the third Tuesday of June, to be opened by Rev. Barnabas King.

It was also ordered that with these two Presbyteries and the Presbytery of Montrose the

SYNOD OF NEWARK.

be erected to meet on the third Tuesday of October, and to be opened with a sermon by Asa Hillyer, D. D.

The Presbytery of Rockaway had at its organization, chiefly in Sussex and Morris Counties, sixteen ministers and fifteen churches and brought into the Presbytery of Morris and Orange at reunion eighteen ministers, twenty churches and 2230 communicants. The chief churches of Rockaway Presbytery in 1870 were Rockaway, Harmony First, Boonton, Wantage Second, Dover, and Mendham Second.

The Synod of New York and New Jersey was formed by the union of the Synod of Newark and the Synod of New York in 1840.*

REUNION.

In the survey of twenty-five years it seemed needful to sketch in close connection the Presbyteries of both the Old and the Reconstructed Synods. Now let us turn to 1870 and notice the Reunion which made reconstruction possible.

A comparison of the territory of the old and of the new Synod and the relative condition of the churches will help us

---

*See Minutes G. A. (N. S.) 1840, p. 18.

to understand the effects of the Reunion. When the means
of communication between the two great cities New York
and Philadelphia were slow and tedious it was natural that
those cities should be the ecclesiastical as well as the commercial centres for a large scope of surrounding country. Thus
the churches of West or South Jersey were attached to the
Presbytery and Synod of Philadelphia until convinced that
this provincial dependence was not advantageous, when they in-
dependently and boldly undertook to manage their own affairs.
In like manner, the churches of East Jersey gravitated towards
New York, expecting advantage from their metropolitan re-
lations. Since communication through and throughout the
State has become rapid, and since the different sections are
bound more closely together with bands of steel, the tendency
has been to Home-Rule in the Church as well as in the State.

In 1861 the Synod extended hundreds of miles into Pennsylvania * and while in New Jersey it covered nominally the
State with the exception of the Presbyteries of Newark and
Rockaway, yet it had not exclusive Presbyterial jurisdiction
over the territory which it occupied.

CHURCHES OF EXTERNAL PRESBYTERIES.

The Presbytery of *Brooklyn* led by Doctor Samuel H. Cox
established a foreign mission in the Pines of New Jersey at
Manchester in 1842.

At some time during the period from 1840 to 1870

The Presbytery of *New York* had two churches in Jersey
City, the First and the Scotch, and one in Weehawken ;

The Presbytery of *New York Second* had a church at
Tenafly ;

The Presbytery of *New York Third* had two churches in
Jersey City, the Second and Bergen First, and two in Hoboken, the First and the West ;

The Presbytery of *New York Fourth* had a church at
Englewood.

* See Doctor Rodgers' Discourse, page 10.

The Presbytery of *Philadelphia Fourth* had churches at Bethlehem, Belvidere Second, Alexandria First, Beverly, Fairview, Atco, Vineland, Bridgeton Second, Fairfield and Cedarville.

Thus, six Presbyteries which were foreign to the State had twenty churches upon the soil of New Jersey. In the larger towns and cities, side by side were churches under different Presbyteries of the State. Presbyteries were interlocked, with conflict of jurisdiction and jealousies, so that it was difficult for some holding the same standards to dwell together in cordial sympathy, if in apparent peace.

Verily, there was occasion to reiterate our Saviour's prayer for unity, "That they all may be one, that the world may believe that Thou hast sent Me." Some deplored the evils and the difficulty; but how to accomplish a remedy was the super-human problem. Here we raise the monumental inscription,

"Hitherto hath the Lord helped us."

This is the Lord's doing; it is marvellous in our eyes.

REUNION came, followed by RECONSTRUCTION: order sprang out of confusion: harmony out of discord. As in the Church at large so in New Jersey the way was prepared gradually. In October, 1868, the Synod of New Jersey met in the Third Presbyterian Church of Newark and the Synod of New York and New Jersey met in the First Presbyterian church of the same city. The committees on religious exercises of each Synod held a conference together and upon their joint recommendation the two Synods united, first in a meeting for prayer and conference in the Third Church, on Tuesday evening, presided over by the two Moderators, and on the next day the Synod of New Jersey adjourned to meet with the Synod of New York and New Jersey for the purpose of celebrating the Lord's Supper at the First Presbyterian Church in the afternoon.

In the morning of that day and before the communion, the following resolution, offered by Doctor J. H. McIlvaine, was adopted by the Synod of New Jersey:

FIRST PRESBYTERIAN CHURCH, NEWARK, N. J.

Corner Stone laid September, 1787.   Opened for worship January 1, 1791.

Chapel Dedicated June, 1873.

Resolved, That in the judgment of this Synod, such an agreement in doctrine and such a degree of mutual confidence and love now exist between the Old and the New School Branches of the Presbyterian Church as are contemplated in the following resolution of the General Assembly of 1866.

" *Resolved,* That the Assembly expresses its fraternal affection for the other Branch of the Presbyterian Church and its earnest desire for reunion at the earliest time consistent with agreement in doctrine, order and polity on the basis of our common standards and the prevalence of mutual confidence and love, which are necessary to a happy union and to the permanent peace and prosperity of the United Church."

And, consequently that the reunion between the two bodies ought in the judgment of this Synod to be consummated without unnecessary delay *

In the next year, 1869 it was

Resolved, That the Synod of New Jersey in session ⌐at Rahway send fraternal greetings to the Synod of New York and New Jersey in session at Poughkeepsie, N. Y., and rejoice in the coming closer union spiritually and ecclesiastically.

The telegraph on the next day brought the following response:

The Synod of New York and New Jersey in session at Poughkeepsie, N. Y., cordially respond to the Fraternal Greetings of the Synod of New Jersey in session at Rahway, N. J., hoping and believing that the coming union will prove that we are one in Christ Jesus. †

At Elizabeth in 1870 all parts of the two Synods dwelling in New Jersey blended into one Synod and now, like those who are embarked upon a reconstructed ship, sailing towards the open sea—borne onward by prosperous winds, no one of us can tell from the deep blue of the commingled waves

* Minutes of Synod 1868, p. 8. † *Ibid.* 1869, pp. 8 and 16.

whether these came from the Raritan or those from the Passaic.

As we bend our gaze to the voyage which is beyond, let us raise aloft our banner and inscribe upon it—Hitherto hath the Lord helped us—and looking backward upon our course during a quarter of a century notice the progress in *education;* in *systematic beneficence;* in *church extension,* and in *spiritual results.*

EDUCATION AND SUNDAY-SCHOOLS.

It is no new thing for the Presbyterian Church to give attention to the young. In Sunday-schools there has been progress. In 1861 and 1862 a committee of this Synod urged a revision of the Directory for Worship, so as to recognize the true relation of the Session and Pastor to the Sunday-school, and was instructed to address an overture to the General Assembly on this topic.*

The Narratives notice how public services for children; stated preaching to them; catechetical instruction; greater care in selecting libraries; also Sunday-school Institutes, all indicate correct views of the relation of the Sunday-school to the Church and a growing interest in the work.† It should therefore fill us with gratitude rather than with surprise when we hear of fruit gathered from our Sunday-schools and that of twenty-two added to one church, twenty were from the Sunday-school,‡ and of another that all the scholars above twelve years of age are in the communion of the church.‖ So again do we quote with approval the saying, that the lambs of the flock have a right to be marked with the name of the Shepherd who owns them : and repeat the German proverb, that we may appreciate its spiritual meaning, "From the Home to the School; from the School to the Church; from the Church to Heaven."

---

* See MSS. Minutes 1861, p. 259, and *Ibid.* 1862, p. 317.

† Minutes of Synod, 1874, p. 38.   ‡ *Ibid,* 1883, p. 38.

‖ Westminster at Elizabeth, Minutes of Synod, 1875, p. 47.

The relation of the Synod to the College of New Jersey
and to the Theological Seminary at Princeton needs no eluci-
dation here; but Synod, with gratitude, may call to mind the
large endowments, which the Lord has sent from different
quarters to these institutions during the last twenty-five years.

In this same period the German Theological Seminary, now
located at Bloomfield, for the training of ministers to labor
among our German population has come into existence by the
fostering care of the Presbytery of Newark and claims our
sympathy. In 1874 the first class of eight young men was
graduated.

The Narratives frequently mention a work of grace in
academic institutions, as at Bridgeton, Blairstown, Lawrenceville, and other places. It would be a valuable contribution
which shall give the history of Presbyterial Academies and
Female Seminaries established in all the chief towns throughout this Synod.*

BENEVOLENCE AND BENEFICENCE.

There has been a great advance in Christian benevolence
and systematic beneficence. The increase in the number of
the objects is worthy of notice. At the organization of Synod †
the statistical tables contained only five columns for the reports
of contributions. Two of these, The Presbyterial Fund and
The Commissioners were virtually the same, and are now
usually combined under the "General Assembly" column.
Two others, for the Theological Seminary and for Education,
were very similar if not identical; while one *Missionary*
column included all other benevolent contributions. The
columns for missionary and benevolent gifts are now increased
to nine, besides the three columns for the General Assembly,
for Congregational expenses, and the Miscellaneous making
twelve in all. This increase of calls has secured fuller returns
and larger gifts. ‡

---

* See Minutes of Synod 1864, p. 7; 1865, p. 16; 1872, p. 34; 1876, p. 40; 1885, p. 40.

† See Minutes General Assembly, 1825.

‡ See Narratives in Minutes of Synod, 1868, p. 12; 1871, pp. 18 and 20; 1872, p. 32; 1882, p. 22.

The organized efforts of Christian Women, first in behalf of Foreign Missions, and later for Home Missions, have grown with the progress of this quarter of a century.

Synod's own efficient Standing Committee on systematic beneficence has aimed to secure collections from every church to all the Boards; to promote weekly offerings and proportionate giving as well as to increase the aggregate of contributions.

Among the sisterhood of Presbyteries, Morris and Orange is frequently mentioned as setting a noble and notable example. *

Doctor Rodgers in his Historical Discourse gives two interesting points for comparison. He comforts himself with the thought that only two Synods, those of New York and Philadelphia had paid to the Board of Domestic Missions more than the Synod of New Jersey. At the same time he lamented that the Synod of New Jersey was one of the Synods which drew out of the treasury of the Board of Domestic Missions more than it paid into it; for it drew out for its forty-six † missionaries, $6,803.99, and paid in 1861 into the treasury, $6,278.51. In recent years this Synod, by the combined gifts of the churches, its women and its Sunday-schools, has paid to the Board of Home Missions, from $25,000 to $30,000 annually, while in 1885–86 it paid to the Board, $44,904.21, and received from the Board for its fifty-seven missionaries, $9,849.02.‡

---

* See Minutes of Synod, 1873, p. 16; 1875, p. 46; 1883, p. 86.

† Doctor Rodgers also classified the Missionaries in 1860–61 thus:

In the Presbytery of		New Brunswick,	2
"	"	" Elizabethtown,	2
"	"	" Passaic,	1
"	"	" Newton,	5
"	"	" Raritan,	2
"	"	" Luzerne,	13
"	"	" West Jersey,	9
"	"	" Burlington,	3
"	"	" Susquehanna,	6
"	"	" Monmouth,	3

Of whom nineteen or more were in Pennsylvania.   46

‡ See Report of the Board of Home Missions, 1886, pp. 2 and 112.

Doctor Rodgers estimated that the collections of the Synod
for the year 1861 for benevolent missionary and miscellaneous
objects amounted to twenty-five thousand dollars.* In 1862
they amounted to $52,359. The sum of all the contributions
for similar purposes, according to the Minutes of the General
Assembly of 1886, exclusive of congregational expenses,
amounted to $327,610, adding for congregational expenses
$688,443, we have a total of $1,016,053.† If sometimes
we complain and urge our churches to do more, it is also fitting
when we notice an advance from tens to hundreds of thousands, and even a million, that we commend the liberality of
those who have done so much.

---

*Synod contributed in the year 1860–61:

To the Board of Domestic Missions,	. . . . . .	$6,278 51
"	" Foreign Missions, ...	8,128 43
"	" Education, ...	2,652 76
"	" Publication, ...	1,362 81
"	Church Extension Committee, ...	1,386 47

Total to five Boards, . . . $19,808 98

Adding money given to the Disabled Ministers' Fund, the Bible, Tract and Sunday-
school, and other institutions, Doctor Rodgers says, " We may safely estimate the
collections of the year at $25,000. Historical Discourse, p. 24.

† CONTRIBUTIONS OF SYNOD OF NEW JERSEY.

See Minutes of General As-sembly, in	To Benevolence and General Assembly and Miscellaneous	To Congre-gational Expenses.	Total.
1862	52,359	$163,285	$215,584
1871	197,840	748,638	946,478
1885	222,987	687,468	910,455
1886	327,610	688,443	1,016,053

Contributions reported in 1886, in Minutes of General Assembly.

To the Board of Home Missions	$87,665
Foreign Missions	81,399
Education	11,942
Publication	4,458
Church Erection	¶ 58,702
Ministerial Relief	11,043
Freedmen	9,660
Sustentation	2,297
Aid for Colleges	5,000
General Assembly	5,509
Miscellaneous	49,935
	$327,610

¶ Includes $45,000 for a single church. See Minutes of Synod, 1886, p. 49.

The special and grand memorial offerings following Reunion belong to this period. In 1871 the contributions for congregational expenses being affected probably by memorial offerings were greater than in 1886; but the contributions for all other objects have largely increased.

CHURCH EXTENSION AND HOME MISSIONS.

Hitherto the Lord has helped the Synod in the work of Home Missions and Church Extension. In some large cities, as Newark especially, but not there alone, mission schools have resulted in large accessions of members and sometimes have grown into new churches. Some churches have employed a female missionary to lead in Mothers' Prayer Meetings; in Helping Hand Societies; in Industrial Schools; to report the worthy poor, and to visit from house to house.*

In olden times, as with the voice of a clarion, Thomas P. Hunt proclaimed the wants and predicted the growth of the great missionary field in the coal regions of Pennsylvania, and in comparison, the Pines of New Jersey were lightly esteemed. After reconstruction, when the Synod and the State became conterminous, the Synod turned its attention to the southern half of the State. It had been diligently cultivated by John Brainerd, more than a century ago; but after the Revolutionary War had been too long overlooked. It is difficult for strangers to understand how there can be missionary ground in a State so old and so highly favored as New Jersey. They have not known how large a portion of southern New Jersey has been a wilderness of pines. Thirty-three years ago there were no railroads in the southern half of the State, excepting the one line, via Amboy from Philadelphia to New York. Since that time, and mainly within a quarter of a century, five hundred miles of railroad have been constructed, reaching to every important town and all along the coast. By thus increasing the facilities of transportation;

---

* See Minutes of Synod, 1874, Appendix, pp. 38, 39 and 40, and 1877, p. 68.

by opening to settlement large tracts of land, which had been practically inaccessible ; by establishing many sea side resorts ; by the consequent increase of population ; by all these results, the southern portion of New Jersey has been revolutionized and the Synod has realized, none too soon, that it has here an important and inviting field for Church Extension.

It was in 1872, and after reunion was an accomplished fact, that a resolution was adopted for the appointment of a standing committee to consider the condition and prospects of Church Extension and Home Missions, and to report annually the need and progress of this work. That resolution fell unobserved, like one of the smallest of seeds, and no one foresaw to what proportions it would grow. The next year, 1873, at Washington, the committee presented an extended report, which opened the way for enlarged and successful efforts for church extension, as published in the reports of the committee for each succeeding year. It was a remarkable providential coincidence that without any preconcert between the writers of the two reports, the narrative of the same year, 1873, concluded with an eloquent and unusual argument for the thorough evangelization of the State of New Jersey. *

STATISTICS AND GROWTH.

It is impossible to make a comparison of statistics for twenty-five years at all satisfactory, because of the great and entire change of territory and boundaries. It will be sufficient to prepare a table of statistics at different epochs.† The growth of the Synod will appear by a comparison of these periods: 1823, 1861, 1886. A full attendance of every minister and one elder from each church would have made in 1823, a Synod of only 187 members ; and in 1861, a Synod of 379 members; and would now make, including Corisco, an assembly of 680 ministers and elders, thus:

	Ministers.		Churches.		Total.
In 1823,	83	+	104	=	187
" 1861,	185	+	194	=	379
" 1886,	391	+	289	=	680

* See Minutes of Synod, 1873, pp. 18-20. † See p. 32.

COMPARISON OF 1871 AND 1886.

It is not difficult to obtain reliable statistics of the reconstructed Synod for the last *fifteen* years, during which its territory has been unchanged.   From 1871 to 1886 the nine Presbyteries continuing the same, the ministers have increased from 310 to 391; the churches from 237 to 289; and communicants from 37,912 to 50,302, a net increase of 81 ministers, 52 churches, and 12,390 communicants in fifteen years.

Year.	Presbyteries.	Ministers.	Churches.	Communicants.	Congregational Expenditures.
1871, ...	9	310	237	37,912	$748,638.00
1886, ...	9	391	289	50,302	688,443.00

SPIRITUAL RESULTS.

Omniscience alone can estimate the spiritual results of labor during a quarter of a century.   Success, or growth, or usefulness is not always nor alone to be measured by professed conversions.   A few added to a small church may be more effective and valuable *relatively* than the many added to a larger church. · But to preach the Gospel to every creature; to proclaim the doctrines of grace and to offer a free salvation to perishing sinners through the atonement of our Lord and Saviour Jesus Christ is our chief, and should be our constant aim.

The earliest years of the period under review were years of excitement and of civil war.   It is not surprising to read in the Narratives, such words as these: "There has been no great awakening.*   Most of the Presbyteries lament barrenness and worldly-mindedness, an increase of Sabbath desceration and intemperance;"† and yet the Narrative of 1863,‡ makes mention of some ingathering, and while in 1864 there was no general revival of religion, nearly all the churches reported some additions.   Similar to this was the tone of the Narratives for 1865, and 1867, and 1868.

The Narrative of 1866 reviewing the preceding year said,

---

* MSS. Minutes of Synod, 1861, p. 256.   † *Ibid.*, 1863, p. 349.   ‡ *Ibid.* p. 283.

"Already there was seen to be a corruption of morals. Crime was fearfully prevalent; gigantic frauds were perpetrated by men of high position; suddenly acquired wealth had begotten luxurious and profligate manners hitherto unknown in our republic; mammon and fashion were leading the people in a carnival of ungodliness, and the piety of the Church did not seem vigorous enough to stem this flood of irreligion and vice. The only hopeful sign was that God's children recognized the peril and bemoaned their own supineness. The Church throughout the land felt that help was in God alone, and the prayer everywhere was 'Turn us again, O God, and cause Thy face to shine, and we shall be saved.' The Lord heard and answered prayer, and this Synod has shared in the general religious awakening, which will render the winter of 1865–66 memorable in the annals of the Church." *

Then followed a few years of adjustment to the new condition of things, and a general spirit of prosperity, with some special manifestations of grace. Very cheerful and sanguine was the Narrative of 1870.

The year 1876 was the most signal year of revival in the history of the Synod, and 4,518 souls were reported as added on examination. Of these 974 were added to the Presbytery of Monmouth, which is believed to have been in that year, the largest number in proportion to its membership of any Presbytery of our denomination in the United States. †

For nine years, from 1862 to 1870 inclusive, the additions on examination in the Synod were 12,241, an average of 1,360 per year.

For the sixteen years, from 1871 to 1886 inclusive, the additions on examination have been 36,978, an average of 2,311 per year.

Whatever may be the cause, or however affected by change of territory or methods, or by increase of population, the average annual additions, on examination, since 1871 have

---

* Minutes of Synod, 1866, p. 8.

† See Doctor Aikman's Report, Minutes of synod, 1876, p. 64.

been nearly twice as many as they were before the reunion. In all these things hitherto the Lord hath helped us. Praise be to His Name, who permits us to be in some small measure co-workers with Him.

CONCLUSION.

We would not forget the claims of other portions of our common country; nor ignore the work of other Denominations, yet do we owe as a Synod a special responsibility to this State, which is peculiarly committed to our care.

New Jersey, the thirty-fifth in area and the nineteenth in population, is the seventh in rank in the product of mines; the sixth in the product of manufactures; the first in the means of communication by railroads and canals, and has been foremost in the valuation of farm lands, and in the value of products per acre.

Peculiarly important is its position between the two great cities, from which multitudes come to find among us their homes. It is a highway for a large part of the traffic from the South and West; is rapidly increasing in wealth and population and seems to be destined to become the most densely populated State in the Union.

In cultivating this field the Presbyteries need the sympathy and fostering care of the entire Synod; for we are ecclesiastically one body, and the eye cannot say unto the hand, I have no need of thee; nor again the head to the feet, I have no need of you, and whether one member suffer all the members suffer with it, or if one member be honored all the members rejoice with it. *

With a compact territory we are one body. Let it be our endeavor, depending upon the Divine blessing, to cultivate this territory for our Lord and Saviour Jesus Christ.

The church is compared to a body having many members. Let us so think of our Synod as a symmetrical body and its Presbyteries as members one of another.

---

* 1 Cor. 12: 21–26.

It is vital to the human body that the lungs and heart be
in normal condition; so is it essential to the life of the Synod
that New Brunswick, central as its heart, shall ever be faithful and sound. With Jersey City on the East and Elizabeth
on the West, our fair Synod stretches forth her hands to
draw from other States commercial and mineral wealth. At
Newark she opens her mouth and words of eloquence and
unction fall from her lips. Under the brow of overhanging
hills, through the eyes of Morris and Orange, she looks joy-
ously over her fruitful fields. Newton, as the head, serenely
crowns the whole body; while Monmouth and West Jersey,
with willing feet, stand ready to extend the domain of our
fair Synod. Comprising eight Presbyteries here, and not for-
getting our little Sister far away Corisco, truly we are one
Synod, one united body and members one of another.

Therefore, let there be no schism in the body; but let the
members have the same care one for another. While we
maintain the unity of the body let us strive to maintain the
unity of the Spirit in the bond of peace.

Note.—The writer acknowledges his debt to Doctor Rodgers for much
valuable information, without which it would have been impossible to have
prepared this discourse. In recounting the origin of the earlier Presbyteries he has aimed to interweave in this narrative the essential items
for the benefit of those to whom Dr. Rodger's work is not accessible.

Besides giving an exposition and application of his text, Dr. Rodgers
gave obituary notices of four Ministers who had died in the preceding
ecclesiastical year, viz.: Revs. Messrs. Isaac V. Brown, D. D.; Nicholas
Murray, D. D.; John Dorrance, D. D.; and Thomas Spencer Ogden, a
missionary to Corisco. He also reported, that from 1823 to 1860 inclusive, there had been in the several Presbyteries, while connected with
the Synod:

Ordinations 273
Installations 236
Dismissions to other Presbyteries and other bodies . . . 380
Dissolution of the Pastoral relation 267
Licensed to preach 470
Churches organized 126
Clerical members removed by death, including the
four above mentioned 73

In 1882 the Synod became a Corporate body, having filed a certificate
with the Clerk of the County of Essex, and adopted as the Corporate Name
THE TRUSTEES OF THE SYNOD OF NEW JERSEY.

PRESBYTERY	Year	Ministers	Churches	Communicants	Congregat'nal Contributions
New Brunswick, . . .	1738				
	1823	23	15	1480	
	1861	42	20	4663	$ 41,623
	1870	46	23	5121	49,745
	1886	64	33	7146	87,679
Raritan, ...	1840	9	14	1260	
	1861	10	15	1743	8,013
	1870	19	18	2381	56,678
Newton, ...	1819	14	25	1515	
	1823	18	31	2398	
	1861	27	30	3985	28,039
	1870	31	28	3832	54,417
	1886	38	35	5504	57,461
Elizabethtown, ...	1825	17	16	3162	
	1861	26	16	2991	20,265
	1870	32	17	3231	60,950
Elizabeth, ...	1871	43	29	5283	120,438
	1886	49	32	7093	106,838
West Jersey, ...	1839	12	13	1085	
	1861	15	22	2044	16,422
	1870	23	28	2980	47,688
	1886	44	45	5432	77,934
Monmouth, ...	1860	12	12	1436	7,377
	1861	11	12	1490	8,763
	1870	15	13	1870	20,648
	1886	49	44	5058	53,250
Burlington, ...	1849				
	1850	6	8	199	
	1861	10	13	791	5,268
	1870	11	14	1190	14,535
Corisco, ...	1860				
	1861	4	1	66	66
	1870	4	2	89	26
	1886	9	7	674	111
Newark, ...	1825	20	19	3025	
	1839	30	29	3210	
	1861	41	23	5461	
	1870	58	35	8104	138,444
	1871	38	22	5816	
	1886	50	25	7555	133,232
Jersey City, ...	1871	32	21	3357	69,652
	1886	38	29	4597	76,524
Morris and Orange, . .	1871	36	31	5109	99,275
	1886	50	39	7243	95,414
Rockaway, ...	1839				
	1840	16	15	704	
	1861	22	20	2334	
	1870	18	20	2230	27,740
Passaic, ...	1853	17	14	2635	22,489
	1861	18	14	2957	24,814
	1870	29	19 ·	3662	116,939

The Publishers of the *New York Evangelist*, issued a Map of the Synod of New Jersey after the Reunion. Sixty changes have been made in the original Electroplate to reproduce the Map in this present form. It exhibits the relative position and size of the PRESBYTERIES and the name of every place, where there is one, or more than one, *regularly organized* Presbyterian Church.——1888. A. H. B.

NEW YORK

PENNSYLVANIA

J E R S E Y   C I T Y

NEWARK

ORANGE

M O R R I S

S U S S E X

W A R R E N

E L I Z

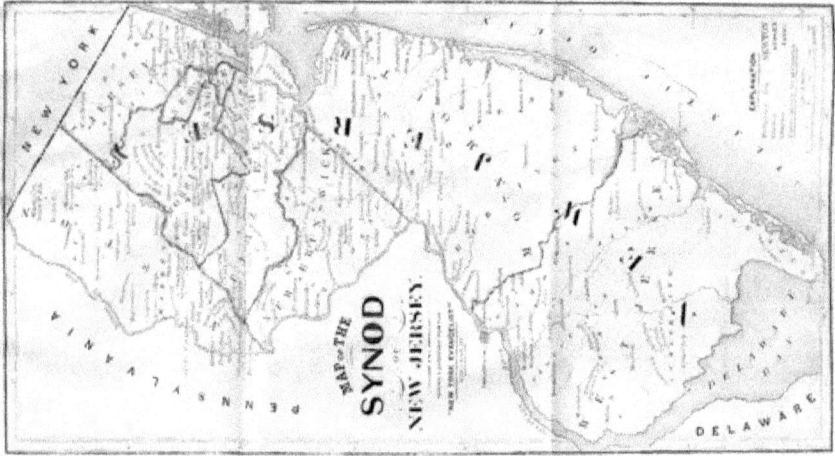

MAP OF THE
SYNOD
OF
NEW JERSEY

www.ingramcontent.com/pod-product-compliance
Lightning Source LLC
Chambersburg PA
CBHW021634270326
41931CB00008B/1019